Distant Love

Distant Love

"Receiving Your Adoration Is Beyond Better Than Dreaming."

TELESHA JUNOR

To order additional copies of this book, contact:
Xlibris
1-888-795-4274
www.Xlibris.com
Orders@Xlibris.com
740703

CONTENTS

Dedication

....

This poetry book is a dedication to my husband who I love sincerely from the start. Our journey has been a bitter sweet one yet tremendous and special. I don't ever want the magical spark between us to cease.

Acknowledgement

....

A huge appreciation to my dear family and friends who have read my poems over the years. Thank you for your compliments and positive feedback.

Miles Apart

Although we are thousands of miles apart,
I can see your face each day.
I can see the love in your eyes,
And the trust in your smile,
I can feel your arms around me.

Although we are thousands of miles away,
I will continue to hope and pray.
I will always express that I love you,
And that I miss you deeply.

Although we are far apart,
It's not too far at all.
The thousands of miles between us,
That's all it will ever be.

I Wonder

Like the flowers that bloom together,
I wish we had the same bond.
To grow side by side endlessly until our time has come.
Like two plants far apart, we stand alone.
Sometimes I wonder when our roots will be inseparable.
With all the sunlight received,
I want us to breathe the same air.
As I sit calmly and wonder about life,
I wonder what it might have been without you,
And what our future is yet to bring.
I wish for our son to have your eyes and
our daughter to have my smile.
It would give us joy to be shoulder to shoulder.
You have shaped years of my life into something special,
And that I value as the years go by.
In you I see my future, my clover that will stand very close.
In you I see strength, the source of motivation to guide my path.
At times I wonder how your heart bears my lengthy absence.
Possibly like the way my heart bleeds for
your warm and tender care.
One of a kind you are; no one else like you I will ever find.
No one else like you will I ever wonder about.
You are the one I place in the centre of my thoughts.

Long Distance Love

I am here and you are there.
Such a huge commitment because we are not near.
Trusting and adoring,
Our key to growth along with honesty.
One may ask why but we seek a way how.
Insecure we are at times and lonely;
However, passionate and committed.
The distance between seems like a test.
Weeks became months and months became years.
We still continue to hold strong.
The hills, the valleys and the ocean between us won't be forever.
Our hearts feel destined together.
To part from you my long distance love, is not an option.
You are my dove, my angel; the purest one.
The one I love and will cherish till the end of time.

Hold You

My heartbeat,
My true prince,
Rescue me with your sword right now.
Save me, embrace me and satisfy my every need.
My sunlight,
My lifeline,
Come with your strength right now.
To heal me, adore me and complete my one wish.
I wish to hold you this minute.
Show you what I missed.
My charmed one,
My true half,
I long to hold you tight,
To kiss you, caress you and never let you go.

My One and Only

Whenever I think of you, my heart fills with joy and happiness.
My thoughts run wild exploring our journey.
Being apart, those memories are like calm piano melodies.
Plays beautifully over and over.
Each note strikes a significant piece to our steps forward.
The phone calls are reminders of your love.
Especially to hear the sweetness in your voice;
It puts a bright smile on my face.
I can't help myself but to appreciate you,
love you and make you happy.
Through the good times and the bad, I know you will be there.
That is one reason why I love you so much.
You help me to flourish.
You help me to mature with you.
You have opened my eyes to a lot in life.
Having you as my right hand man means the world to me.
My one true love.

I love you

If I were to be trapped by the deep ocean waves,
Or by the shallow sea waters,
The roars of the waves would not prevent you from jumping in.

If I were to be in any emotional state,
Or simply need someone to talk to,
You would be at the end of the phone line comforting me.

I remember you saying "it is my job."
It is what you signed up for.
I am truly glad to have you in my life.

At this moment in our relationship,
I have a strong faith in our future goals.
I know where your heart is.

If you could fulfill all my needs and wants,
I know I would receive them willingly.
I am delighted to be your true half.
Just don't ever forget that I will always, always love you.

In Love

Deeply I've fallen.
Although you are so far away,
Often times, words are scarce to utter.
The odd feeling I found myself in.
The gratitude to be loved by another;
More fondly than ever.
Gaining as much love as I offer.
I love you my precious one.
I am delighted that I said "yes."
Your love comes effortless yet pure.
You are my all.
You are the one I adore.

Like a Dove

Like a dove,
You have showered me with your love.
Like a gentleman, you are my right hand man.
Like a heart needs a beat,
That is how badly I need you.
With our dreams, we gave each other hope.

Like a dove,
You have showered me with your love.
Like a star, you shine so bright.
Like a true friend, you will shine to the very end.
For a brighter tomorrow, we will shine always.
With our faithfulness, we are more devoted.

Like a Puzzle

Being together is like building a puzzle,
With each piece, they become one.
Similar to how you and I have bonded.
The moments we share are like the puzzle pieces put together.
The more pieces we connect, the stronger our puzzle.
Same as how our love for each other grows.
Piece by piece the clearer the picture.
The more we realize that we are meant to be.
It's amazing how we have continued to
cherish the puzzle we have created.
Our puzzle is more than half way finished.
I promise to not let the pieces we built fall apart.
I will always love you.
In the struggles of matching the pieces and even when we get it right.

Meeting Once More

Patience is not my current virtue,
Each day left is like a countdown for me.
My mind overflows with thoughts of only you,
And us meeting once more.
I keep thinking of us kissing under the sun.
And making love under the moon.
I am surely touched by you.
The days are going by as quick as they can,
But my anxiousness believes not quickly enough.
Tonight I will be thinking of you before I lay to rest,
And also when I rise at dawn.
I will be seeing your picture on my phone each day.
Hearing your voice over the phone,
Which makes me wish I was there with you.
I miss you so much it hurts to be apart.
Soon I will see you and there will be joy in my heart.
Lots of hugs and kisses are yet to come.

Sex on the Beach

As the sun went down, the moon came out.
Shining bright as it slowly moved across the sky.
The beautiful stars above twinkle hello.
Rushing waves of the sea heads calmly to shore.
We cuddled together on the white sand bed.
Holding hands as we gaze into the restful sky.
The cold breeze from the sea gave me chills,
I drew closer and closer,
The gentleness of his hands soothes my being.
The tension in my body was long gone.
I feel no stress; it's just you and I together at last.
We kissed, talked and laughed,
Surely, I found myself superior to you.
I wanted you greatly;
Impatient I was to disrobe my garb.
I could see it in your eyes;
The fervour; the loving you were about to give.
Passionate yet heated; the chills were all gone.
If we were seen by another, we would have not known.
We were in our own world.
Happy as can be.
Enduring months of no bodily contact,
We finally got to be in each other's arms.

Room for Two

A brown footing furnished wood was opened,
And there I got a welcome on the cheek.
Step by step inside, I glanced at the room.
A room remodelled and adorned for two.

The pink roses lined on the floor led me,
And the palms on my torso shields and own me.
Towards the diner, I saw a two portion meal,
Just a warm and relaxed room set for two.

With a delightful scent from lit candles,
And an amazing song full of mellow for two.
We rambled to the furniture spread over with sheets,
And then enjoy this room set for two.

Find Me

You found me,
Friended me and made me your love.
You kissed me, caressed me and held me right.
Don't let go because I need you always to feel alright.

Cherish me,
Mould me and guide me along the way,
Look me in the eyes and let us jump the broom together.
Promise that you will be faithful because
without you I am incomplete.

Please don't forget me, while we are far apart.
Already I am caught up in your magical love of art.
It will hurt deeply to see us fade.
You found me, adored, don't let it be for a while.
Say you will forever be.
My one true match.

I Believe

I believe that you and I were meant to be.
I believe that you will set my troubles free.
I believe that our bond cannot be broken nor faded.
I believe that our love has built a solid wall.
Loving you is what I adore,
And I can happily say "I am sure."
For all the times spent searching, I believe that
I have finally found the love of my life.

I Miss You

Sweetheart I miss you.
Your presence will forever be my strength.
You will forever not be forgotten.
You are the one who often puts a smile on my face.
Your voice, your words, and your smile keep me happy.
Everything about you brings joy to my heart.
Without you in my presence, I am incomplete.
Without you I am not one.
Your absence prevents my mind from resting.
Your comfort is what I truly missed.
Until we are face to face, my feelings remain.
I miss you.

The Way

I love the way you walk.
I love the way you talk.
I love the way you admire me.
It shows how devoted you are.

You always tell me you love me.
You tell me how much you miss me.
You tell me you won't leave,
And all of that reassures me.

I love the way you love me.
I adore the way you care.
I greatly enjoy the way you touch me,
And even when you stroke my hair.

The way you embrace me,
The way you kiss me,
The way you caress me,
I LOVE IT ALL.

The Star You Are

A star that shines bright, guides you all the way.
A star that shines dull fades away from you each day.
When I first met you, you were shining so bright.
Even now you continue to light up my heart.
In the future, I know you will be there,
Because that is the type of star you are.

I Want You

Day and night,
It's like my mind and body are having a fight.
You have me thinking about the first night.
How fulfilling you made me feel,
How connected we were sultrily,
Now that I am nowhere near you,
I wish that my imaginations were real.
Whenever I am with you, I am floating on clouds.
Drifting where ever our actions take me.
Your world is so much better.
Under your dome I wish to be momentarily.
Captivated by your loving.

Sweet Loving

All that I fantasize affects every inch of my earthly being.
Emotionally, I am weak by the sensual
loving you imprinted in my mind.
All that I envision are the desires of sweet loving I long to receive.
Like the rainless desert, my body thirsts for your loving.
Whenever you see me,
Embrace me,
Kiss thy lips and revive the blood flow of my veins.
Whenever you see me,
Grasp me tight,
Caress me gently and erase all my taunting pains.
Whenever I see you, holding you will not be all,
Because I crave daily to have you entirely.
I yearn for my body to be glued to yours
That hours will come and go.
Surely, the lust I endure inside will lure me next to you.
Breathe on my neck and believe that your
wife was missing you badly.
Touch the most sensitive spots on my body and take me high.
Provide me with the pleasurable pain I have been longing for.
I need your sweet loving.
I am weak by these daydreams but I want to be even weaker.
For the loving you give is painful yet sweeter than honey.

It's painful when you are not near

I hate how much I love you.
I hate how much I care.
It hurts my heart deeply.
It is indeed painful when you are not near.
My body cries for you.
My heart aches for you.
My arms beg to hold you close.
It is painful when you are not here.
My lips are longing for your kisses.
I am drowning in thousands of wishes.
Days became weeks,
Weeks became months,
A year feels like forever.
I love you.
I care about you.
It is just hard when you are not near.

I close my eyes

As I close my eyes and let my thoughts run wild.
All that I really think about is you.
When will I ever see you again?
When will I get to cling to you tight?
When will our lips meet once more?
If I were to wish upon a star,
My wish would be to have you closer in my life.
These nights I close my eyes, lonely and
yearning for your good night kisses.
I can only think, hope and wait.
I will forever dream, especially about you my darling,
Because within you my love is destined.

Heart

Heart of joy,
Heart of love,
I am your angel. You are my dove.
Heart of sadness,
Heart of pain,
My love for you still remains.
If you cry, I will cry with you.
If you are ever down, I will lift you up.
My heart desires your heart's needs.
My heart tells what your heart feels.
Heart of joy,
Heart of love,
You are my angel and I am your dove.

The love you have for me

Hearing you speak,
It's like listening to an angel sing.
Passionately singing from your heart,
Genuinely reassuring me of your devotedness,
Each and every day you shine.
Time after time you make me smile,
Because the love you have for me is pure.
The trust, the chemistry and the openness,
they all count.
All of them you deliver.
Day after day.
The love you have for me comes natural.
It is real.
It is not rehearsed.
It is solid and never ending.
And that is what drew me closer to you.

You Promised

You promised to be true,
Being you,
All the way through.

You promised to be forever,
Being there,
Showing you care.

You promised to be my shield.
The one to hold in time of heal,
And I truly see that you meant every word.

Without you

Without you in my life,
It will be hard to move on.
My heart will be broken.
My body will be so numb.

Without you in my life,
I will be forever lost.
My hopes will be shattered.
My comfort will be no more.

Without you in my life,
My source of strength will be gone.
My days will become nights.
And my nights will be rainy.

Without you in my life,
That is a dream I will never wish for.
Because you are like the air I breathe,
And without you I cannot live.

Too Far

You are one phone call away.
For that I am fortunate.
Appreciated and grateful for such opportunity,
But I truly wish you were a foot step away.
So that when I stretch my hands forward our fingers meet.
But that wish is presently hard to attain.
Too far we are.
Others wonder what we gain.
And if it will really last.

Your Presence

Without your presence I am weak at heart.
My mind aches; overflowing with wishes.
My body trembles like a thin leaf in the wind.
My eyes intensely trail tears down to my bosom.
It is very lonely without you.
The boredom causes my head to ache.
No one can make me feel better but you.
Not even souls can do.
In your presence I could smile and I could laugh.
I am sad right now because I miss you badly.
How do I gain strength when you are not here?
How can I laugh when this feeling is no joke?
How can I feel joyful when you are nowhere near?
My love, my life, I wish to see you.
When will I ever get to kiss those sweet lips of yours?
My groom, my charm, I feel unlucky right now.
When this feeling is gone,
I hope the reason is because you are at my door.
No one will I ever love like this.
Your presence is what I desire strongly.

With my eyes close

Each moment I reminisce about you,
I am present in a fantasy land.
A site filles with distress and warmth.
All my desires appears real,
And my discomfort is relief by your love.
With my eyes close, I can almost feel you near.
My mind is at ease through your devoted care.
I sense happiness by the sight of your grin,
And because of your serenity, I feel secure.
Without a doubt, I know that you adore me.
But I sense your compassion to please me even more.
Your weakness for me is like a flower without a stem.
Without each other, we cannot attain growth.
We need each other to bloom beautifully.
With my eyes close, I can feel grateful.
What I have been longing for is not miles away,
But within my heart and the memories you gave me.
Just by a single thought, you are only a heartbeat away.
I feel embraced by your everlasting care.
I sense each move you make and every breath you take.
No one else will I ever connect with like this,
Because my love has boundaries which are only devoted to you.

My Day

A day without you is like a day without sunlight.
There is no sunset for me at dawn.
With no rays of joyfulness, my day begins dull,
Dark like an empty enclosed room,
Trapped, no merriment, cold and lonesome.

I lay around with an unfeeling heart,
Unfilled in the stomach but still I waited.

Waited for your call to shine a beam on my face;
Waited for your jests.

I would love for my days to be as pleasant as your smile,
And for it to be joyful like the laughter we share.
A day without light is not a day at all.
What I need is your company always, and that will light up my day.

A Flower

Imagine a flower without its parts.
Leaves falling to the ground,
Picture how fragile the pedals would be.
And how its stem bent in distress.
This is my vision after we fought.
We became so fragile.
To the least rain drops that hit us.
We focus more on making our points be heard.
We even make the ordeal more complex.
This flower without its parts was once perfect.
It is hard enough that we are far apart.
Why do I see our leaves falling to the ground?
Why is our flower not beautiful today?
I wonder at times if you see what I perceive.
I wonder if you believe I don't understand what you perceive.
All I want again is the beauty of our precious bloom.
Such sight will make me smile once more.

The Sun

As the sun rose one dawn,
I was awakened by its scorching light.
With my face still blue from the past night,
I covered myself from the sunlight.
I did not want a smile to be shone on my face.
I wanted not to rise with the sun or even see its beauty.
And so my mind began to roam.
Wondering the same things it had pondered few hours before.
I wanted it to end.
Why did we argue?
Why did we yell?
Those questions rang in my ears like a bell.
Out of anger, we voiced back and forth.
But I wish the sun was shining last night.
To brighten our thoughts and erase all dark clouds,
Hence, we would not have rained such dark ugly words.
Now my pillows are soaked from my tearful night.
It was like a rain cloud positioned over my head.
I pray for the sun to shine at all times but not just yet.
I want to lay myself to rest and make up for the hours I did not nest.
Sunrise, sunlight, set yourself far from thee but
I will rise soon to greet you at noon.

You

Each day I think of you,
I reminisce of the past,
I dreamt of our future.
The life we live; we share together.
Our love and trust is equally reciprocal.
Nothing else could I ever ask for.
You have completed my dream.
Your heart is filled with enough love for me and more.
All is evident within you.
I chose you and you chose me.
I strongly believe that we were meant to be.
In my heart, you will forever have a place.
A place with endless love and care.
I love you now.
I will love you tomorrow.
I will love you until the very end.

Lonely nights

As I lay my body to rest,
I composed an image of you being at arm's reach.
My lonely nights are tremendously blue.
I drown myself into thoughts of being next to you.
It's uncontrollable thinking of what we have built.
Moments like this I wish could quickly fade away.
I would gladly yearn for your loving and promptly receive it.
Instead of wishing to be held, your arms are already embracing me.
Instead of wishing to be kissed, your warm
lips are already glued to mine.
Rather than pondering about love making,
we would be making love abundantly.
I missed every moment of your presence and your sweet loving.
My lonely nights and lengthy days reflect that.
The sadness in my heart is unbearable at times.
But the moments of you endures within me.
The joyful moments we shared,
Those are the ones that keep me thinking.
It may lead to a tearful night but it would
not be unless I did not love you.
It would not be unless I did not care.
Furthermore, it is because I miss you.
I crave for you each night to make them unforgettable,
Some nights I feel unloved because of the
absence of your physical warmth.
I adore you deeply and I know you feel the same about me too.
The distance between us is the only conflict.
Until that distance becomes shortened, my nights will continue to
be lonely after you whisper the words "I love you and good night."

You are always there

All the pain I bear for you,
All the tears I shed for you,
All the love I have for you,
Were not in vain.

You know how much I love you,
You know how much I care,
You always feel what I am feeling,
Because you were always there.

You promised to be true,
Being you, all the way through.
You promised to be forever,
Being there, showing your care.
You promised to be my shield,
The one to hold in time of heal,
I can truly say that you were being you.

Love

Love a little, it may last short.
Love a lot, it may last long.
Love a bit, there is no love.
Try to love, still no love.
With your heart, you love me.
With your heart, you give freely.

I love you and you love me.
Abundant loving directly from our hearts;
True loving that is,
To ensure it will forever be.

Be Mindful

Be mindful that I love you.
Consider how much I care.
For thy pain and anger are difficult strains to bear.
Whenever my mouth flames, I meant not to share.
I dislike being the cause of having your heart tear.

Be mindful that I am jealous,
And even how much I fear,
For thy time with you is too precious to share.
Whenever my heart breaks, I ask that you will draw near.
For already I despise the misery of not having you here.

Apart

To nurture our emotions, we endlessly hug in warmth.
To show our love and affection, we passionately kiss time after time.
We are devoted to hold the hands of each
other to show that we are one.
And we walk together in comfort and delight.
Our bond is real but all of those we do less
because we spend more time apart.

To put life's pieces together, we converse daily.
To display reassurance of how much we care, we share a smile.
We may show a frown whenever we shift from ups to downs,
But we stick together, because we understand each other.
All of those we do more as we spend time being apart.

Without our minds, memories of us side by
side would not be remembered.
Without vision, our webcams would not be needed.
Without our voice, it would not be the same over the phone.
Without our grasp of love, loyalty and
faithfulness would not be transparent.
And so we are thankful for the connection we have.
Although we are apart, our dream still remains.

It Feels so Right

For better, for worst,
In sickness and in health,
Till death do us part,
I will always be there.
Love, trust and honesty will do.
Ups and downs are a part of it.
Your smile, your heart,
Your friendship, your love,
You comfort and dreams.
You are everything I want and need.
Let us take one step at a time,
To make this love lasting,
Because when you smile at me,
When you kiss me,
And even when you hold me,
It feels so right.
I could very much see the light.

I Need You

When it rains outside,
My heart realizes how I miss you truly.
The pain I feel; it is something real.
I know it is the same for you.
I miss you; when I need someone to hold.
I need you, I need you.

Because whenever I see them kiss and I see them beam,
I truly wish it was us.
I feel so alone; I can't have you that far.
I got to have you close.

Tearful nights come and go;
I need to see you more.
I cry, I'm weak now.

I miss you when you are out of my reach.
You are the person I see.
I miss you; when I need someone to hold, I got to have you close.
I need you, I need you.

Dreaming of You

From inside out, my body felt weary.
Despite the feeling, I needed an extra hour.
One more sleepless hour to reminisce of you.
My eyes failed but my mind was far away from resting.
Dreaming of you made my night much better.
And so I regret not falling asleep sooner.
My thirst for you is like the need for water.
To quench my thirst I continued dreaming.
You kissed me, I kissed back.
You bit my lips, I repeated your action.
This illusion of you appeared distinctly.
I wanted my eyes to remain closed.
I have endured a long wait for your touch.
I am gladly holding you tight, I am I really dreaming.
You gazed at me; I smiled because this moment is pure healing.
You stroked my hair, I wiped your face.
You kissed me with so much care.
Dreaming of you enables me to love you all night,
But now it's ending as the sun began to rise.

Rescue Me

In the midst of a flame,
I am definitely getting burned.
The pain is excruciating and I am badly in need of help.
All my troubles are multiplying.
And without you by my side, the fire may spread.
I wish for your presence and your physical help at this moment.
Because I am running out of answers I cannot find on my own.
My troubles are a heavy burden.
They started to weigh me down.
The pressure, the heat, I cannot bear it anymore.
Please rescue me from carrying this heavy load.

Streetlights

Along a cold blue street,
Touched by the streetlight's embrace.
Alone in company but accompanied with thoughts of you.
These brightened lamps and I are on a road to nowhere.

Suddenly, the voice of you appeared.
The Streetlight trees talked to me.
They gave exhorted words and wishes of yours.
These brightened lamps showed life and gave hope to somewhere.

I'm guided step by step.
Watched by known and unknown.
Trying bumps in the road.
These bright streetlights and I,
Head held high towards the sky with you in my heart.

I Will Be the One

Despite our soreness and struggles,
Our disagreements and our feuds,
He is still watching over us.
I believe he will carry us through.
He will never let us down.
I have never loved someone the way I love you.
Nor cared about another the way I care about you.
God knows I have caused you to worry at times,
But my apologies will always be shown to reassure you.
My love for you has no boundaries.
Nor do I have any doubts.
Sincerely, I can call you my own.
For you and you only, I will be the one.

Your smile and your laugh

Sometimes I am sad, while other times I am glad.
A frown on my face could be easily erased by you.
I smile because my heart is filled with joy,
especially when I glanced at you.
Immediately I realize that you will be the one to the end.
When I laugh, it is because my heart is overflowing.
Overflowing with the happiness you brought to my life.
Your smile is what causes me to smile at times.
It enables me to feel secure and appreciated.
Your laugh always triggers a reaction from me.
It is thrilling to be alone with you.
It is very sensational to be held by you.
I get chills whenever you place your lips on me mildly.
And even when your hands explore my torso.
I love your smile, your laugh and your touch.
Each promotes happiness and that all I wish for both of us.

Drunk by your love

I am walking on thin air.
Joy fills my heart,
Knowing I will hold you by noon.
Safe and secure,
That is how I will feel.
Deeply spellbound,
Just looking at you.
Your smile, I know will be bright like always.
Triggering a reaction from me.
Fortunate I will feel.
I will be more content.
Although it will be a short visit,
I would rather be next to you.
I will always thirst for your presence,
Your comfort and your love.
Drunk in love we are.
Only for each other.

Times and Times

Times and times I weep, as the pain penetrates deep.
I've been wishing that you were near to mend my biggest fear.
I'm scared to lose you because; I wouldn't know what to do.
It would be too much to handle and I
know my feet would be tangled.

Times and times I smile, because I know that you're still there.
I've been wondering how you last; you're
different from the ones in my past.
I don't want to argue; neither do I want us to fight.
I always think I might lose you but somehow I'm never right.

I see your face each night and even when the morning lights.
I wish to have you here, in every moment of my life.
Times and times I wish that I could never let go of you.
Whenever I see you in my sight.

Hate that I can't hate you when I want to

If I dare myself to remain angry at you,
It simply would not work.
My heart would be broken into pieces as the hours go by.
One day of anger and loneliness is unbearable for me.
Already we are living thousands of miles apart.
I hate that I adore you so much, it refrains me from being bitter.
I can't hate you even if I try,
And I know that you can't either even when you want to.
Being silent on the phone is the furthest we could go.
You truly bring out the best in me.
It is not that I hate how much I love you,
Or hate how much I can't be mad at you.
It is simple a reaction to the change you bring.
A change that allows us to find better reasoning.

A Rocky Road

Although we travel steadily along our path,
We became slightly unstable.
We seem to have come across a rocky road.
As we crossed bumps, they began to multiply.
Awaiting us without sympathy.
Why now? I asked myself.
Wondering if these challenges were destined to be.
I despise challenges yet determined to end this journey,
With you by my side.
And so each conflict I yell, I assume, and I wonder.
This path is more than difficult.
My heart would rather be at peace than to overflow with fury.
This rocky road provides less time for joy.
However creates more time for closure.
It is a pillar for progression in handling our troubles.
I will hate to come across another bump on this journey,
But that is part of me saying the words "I do"
No dispute can block my desire of being with you.
For better, for worst,
In sadness or happiness,
I will always love you.

With You I am Able

Every breath that I take, I inhale your love.
Every second my heart beats, my life with you increases.
Whenever I look in your eyes, I see where my future lies.
Each time I get to hug you, your heart connects to mine.
I see where it wants to be.
I know I want the same.
Each time I pray, you are never forgotten.
Each time you call, I am present in your thoughts.
Every moment you say the words "I love
you," I miss you even more.
I envision that capturing smile of yours.
With you I am able.
Life feels at ease because I know that we are stable.
To put a ring on my finger while we still live apart,
I know that you are greatly in love with me.
I trust you too because I see no reasons not to.
I love you because my heart only wants to be with you.
My heart desires your love forever; therefore,
I will always be by your side.

Back to Life

As I rest my head on your chest, I tried to be strong.
But my tears are heavy to store at this point.
I have come to realized that the two weeks
spent with you have come to an end.
Now we are left to pick up the pieces at a later time.
Unwillingly leaving our agenda incomplete.
If I could spend one more night with you,
it would mean a lot to me.
I would swab my tears and free my mind
from thoughts of us separating.
My troubles would be placed on hold.
I could feel more relaxed while receiving your tender care.
I rather such comfort than going back to life;
back to the reality of us being apart.
I always hope for the opposite of loneliness
but soon this vacation will be over.
Leaving us to wonder, reminisce and to wish.
I truly wish the distance between us was shorter.
I wish for a different battle with you.
Not this battle between having you near or having you far.
Because not having you close always prevails.
So here I come lonely world; back to life, back to reality.
Trying to cope daily with us being apart.
Babes I love you and I will be missing you.
I will call you when I reach.

I Would

If I had the power to cast myself within your presence, I would.
Without hesitation I would snap my fingers
and appear into your arms.
Kissing you immediately to begin making up for lost times.
Continuing what we partially finished the last time.
Nervously hoping for time to remain still.
Because the time we spent apart is the duration I want to fulfill.
If I had the power, my wishes would be a reality.
I could refrain from dreaming and receive you instead.
My eyes would be tear free at nights and I could stop feeling blue.
I wish for the days my lips will get to kiss you freely.
Life without you being close is a hardship I can't bear.
And so I would do anything to have you here.

The Mirror

As I stood there,
I saw a reflection of only you and I.
I scent your cologne all over again.
My body felt a rush each moment you kissed my shoulders,
Even when your hands began to discover.
I heard your comforting words but mostly my voice in bliss.
It all felt like I was present in a romance land.
One so engaging, it had me requesting to stay longer.
But it all ended once my fingers touched the mirror.
I wanted to be sure the reflection of us was true, but they weren't.
Why can I not receive these feelings I crave?
Why can't your appearance in the mirror be real?
I saw your face.
You smiled at me.
You catered to my needs and complied with my deeds.
How else could the mirror have presented such a sure image?
If it is not so, I pray that it will soon be, because
the mirror has set my emotions free.

Complicated

If I were to part from you,
Our status would get complicated.
The years we put in will be lost.
I can never leave you thinking that I have betrayed you.
Although we argue at times, I still love you.
Although we have disagreements, I know that we are dissimilar.
Our disputes are what strengthens our bond.
They invite us to communicate.
Once we ignore those invites, complications may begin.
Being with you creates a special spark in my life.
I would not dream for anyone least nor better.
You are the one I chose to be with.
To make our connection complicated is not my mission.

I Want No Other

Within this love life, our knot has remained unbroken.
I have made a promise and I shall continue to give you my all.
My blindness to your love has fully diminished.
You have opened my eyes to see the beauty in you.
Although we live miles apart, I see no need to search for another.
Being with you completes my dreams and satisfies my needs.
All the things I may want can be gained from you.
I want no other within the picture we have created.
All that we have built together is too strong to fall in vain.
I think of you at all times and all that I have
reminisced is pure happiness.
No one else can make me feel the way I am currently feeling.
After years of being with you, I know my heart wants no other.
You are the sun that shines a graceful smile on my face.
The moon that keeps me calm and relaxed at nights.
And the star I admire and wish upon.
I want you only and no one else.

My Spirit

I blinked once, twice and that was all.
My eyes were eventually sealed like a solid wall.
I laid there peacefully deep in my restless state,
But my spirit was awake seeking for my faith.
It knows that it is you and only you are my faith.
And so it travels freely because of my limitations.
It shall deliver my love; to kiss you
goodnight and pray to God above.
My spirit feints for what my heart feels.
Surely, you are the one who can make our vessels heal.
It is a wonderful feeling as my spirit travels to you.
At last, I am able to see the glowing of your halo.
Your spirit was exploring, seeking for its faith too.
Words cannot explain this joy I am feeling inside.
I am sleeping yet smiling because I am hugged by you.
As I snuggle my pillow, I am glad to be
safe and secure in your arms.
My spirit is sure to feel comfortable and adored by you.
It wishes that when we meet again, it will not be in this form.
As for now, continue to embrace me.
Let sleep tight and rise when it is dawn.

Hope

All that I prayed for is to be settled under the same roof as you.
Forever living in harmony as we challenge what life may bring.
Often times I hope because it seems to guide the way.
It seems to make me believe although things may not go well.
Even so, you are my source of strength whenever I am weak.
Weak as I melt away by any crushed dreams.
All that I mostly do is cling onto past memories of us.
Believing that you are all that I want,
Trusting that you can help produce my desires.
I have never hoped for another, neither to love another.
Because I hope for the best in life and I see you standing at the end.
Although I cry at times; hoping for my wishes to come through,
My heart remains strong because it knows that anything is possible.
I still hope for us to join lips each night and each day.
I hope for the possibility of us walking in the park.
I even hope for us to have dinner daily together.
Hoping is what I do hence my wishes would
not be revolved around you.
My mind travels far sometimes but it shows
me the reality and the unreal.
One thing for sure is that the distance
between us is only a temporary wall,
Because I envision it tumbling down sooner or later.
Till then I will not cease to hope for a closer connection with you.

I Am

You love me unconditionally while I do the same,
I am your queen and you are my king.
My left hand in yours is the essence of God's work.
I see no other for I am with you willingly.
Like a mirror on the wall, you heart tells the truth.
I can stand directly to your face over and over again.
Because I know that you accept me for whom I am.
Like the sun, your presence lights up my being,
And that is something I want not to end.
I would not have known if I didn't meet you.
I would not have known if I didn't love you.
My heart is no longer lurking the dark street for its true match.
But it is longing for its better half to be close.
You are my angel, the one who I am terrified to lose.
Even when I walk alone, I starved without your guidance.
I am who I am but I am less without you here.
I am living but I want us to breathe the same air.
Like two love birds, I want us to chirp together.
Walk together, feast together and even do more.
I am yours so I will wait for that very moment to be in progress.
When we live together, you will no longer be my love distance love,
Simply the love of my life.

Travelling to you

Thou I travel on this aircraft to be with you,
I wish that I was present on a jet plane instead.
To be with you sooner.
Less wondering and wishing;
My mind would be more at ease.
How might I react when I see your face once more?
I started to wonder.
It is such a beauty up here, above the clouds.
Somehow I can see us floating away happily on one of them.
The sunset also captures my sight.
It puts my mind to rest although it's drowning in thoughts of you.
The excitement I am feeling blocks myself from being at ease.
And so I started planning my desires I want to fulfill.
I began to consider possible ways I might approach you.
Will I smile first or shed a thousand tears
of joy upon your shoulders?
Will I hug you then or greet you with a magnetic kiss?
Surely, that moment will soon be experience and even more.
For I yearn to spend some quality time with you my love.
I wish for the ending of this trip to never appear,
And that I may find the strength to carry on if it does.
Because saying goodbye to you is never easy.

Wilted Flower

I was once a wilted flower,
Hidden from the natural light that gives hope to life.
My frame bent bit by bit,
Holding onto thin air above the soil in which I stand,
All there was below;
Droughty soil and adventurous roots turned opposite of me.
It was an unhealthy growth.
Perhaps those roots were not meant for sustenance,
Or maybe I was not their true one.
Thus, our connection shared faded, dusting in the wind.
But what wasn't apparent to me,
Was that you were present by years after years as we experienced life.
Waiting for me to feel the same way you do for me.
I repeatedly told you its best to be friends.
No way would you and I be a grand match.
I was wilted at heart; not ready for more regrets,
But I gave in and despite being sightless,
You helped me to see the beauty of the natural sunlight.
You gave me hope to a better and brighter life.
Unhidden from the clouds to rain upon my withered body.
Within you I trust more and love more,
Because you appreciated me more.
You seem driven to be with me forever.
Resigning abroad; travelling back and forth or not.
If you were to part from me, I will be a deceased flower.
Not withered this time around.

Saying Goodbye

Lay your head on my chest,
Breathe on me as hasty as you want.
It is a nightmare for us again,
Glue your hands to mine until it ends.

I wish we didn't have to,
But it is a toll that we must pay.
Repeatedly until this roller coaster wheels away.

I feel as though we are falling off a bridge momentarily.
Our minds filled with fear.
The tides of the water are forceful yet we are still holding on,
But my flight tomorrow will surely separate us two.

A part of your heart will be taken by me.
Half of mine will be left behind too.
It is sad to say that this is our way.

Saying goodbye is not the end for I shall see your face again.
I despise the travelling back and forth,
But I cannot be away from you too long.
Let us nestle all night and clear our minds of how to say goodbye.
Because I wish this vacation to further continue.

Dear my Husband

Words are not enough to express my gratitude,
Of having you in my life.
I wish I was present with you to demonstrate how badly I miss you.
I know deep down inside my heart, you are the only one for me.
Distance or not, I am satisfied with you.
You being a part of my life has been a great adventure.
I pray that we prosper in life and that our fairy tale continues.
We have been together for years now.
Overjoyed I am to say I see a vast future with you.
Today, August 24, 2012 marks our one year wedding anniversary.
Although we are far apart, it won't hurt to celebrate.
The use of technology will be my close friend to feel closer to you.
I appreciate your strength, your love and your affection.
Without your love, our relationship wouldn't have been the same.
We trust, we understand, we communicate and we listen.
You are my better half and there is no other way to express that.
In three weeks I will be able to physically
express all of my emotions.
I cannot wait to see you.
Happy Wedding Anniversary.
Eventually we will celebrate together.
Cheers to our love and commitment and
may we continue to shine.
Love you!

As Long As We Care

Like the bluest sky on a warm summer evening,
You bring satisfying serenity.
I feel trapped in a maze surrounded by absolute true love.
Before I befriended you, I recall dreaming for someone like you.
Now that I can call you my all, there is no letting go.
What we share is something special which seems lasting.
As long as we care, there is no reason to
fear a separation between us.
Thriving with you till the end is a precept
I will continue to live by.
Living the words and wishes of my heart
is a forever ending journey.
Like the sun that shines always, I will constantly love you.
As long as we care, our love will prosper endlessly.
I feel it and I know it; it will forever be us.
What we share might seem common to
others but we see the uncommon.
I see our connection as special as any other.
But most of all I am glad that despite the distance you
remain caring and you love me unconditionally.

Dear my Wife

I love you now,
I will love you tomorrow.
I will always do because I have been blessed by you,
For that I am humbled to call you mine.
Extraordinary you are, one of a kind.
I have been loved in the past but the love you give is incomparable.
It is like the breath of fresh air that never leaves my side.
Without you in my life, breathing will surely not be the same,
And so I am happy that today it is our wedding anniversary.
Although we are unable to spend it together,
The fact still remains that I love you.
I want to spend a hundred years and more with you.
Devoting my all because you are my special angel.
You have engaged my mind to focus its time thinking of you.
It is simply honest to say I have been captured by your love.
Trapped by your persona and your sensuality.
No one else can mend my brokenness like the way you do.
Happy Anniversary to you my wife.
I hope the years yet to come will be spent with you.

Written by: Shawn Junor

Prayed for

What I had in mind was only an indication.
An illusion far from what actually happened.
Being next to you was like fire against ice.
I was slowly melting.
Liquefied by the intensity of your love.
In your arms, enough was evident.
This was the affection we longed for.
This was the moment we dreamt of night after night.
Lonely and miserable without this bliss of heaven.
I never knew heaven was this low.
Smiles from ear to ear,
Kisses from left to right and centre,
And hugs from all different angles.
Being by your side once more meant the world to me.
Nothing could have erased that joy.
Devoted you are when you held me tight.
Caring for my every need.
This was what I prayed for each night,
Because receiving your adoration is better than wishing.

I Live for You

For you and only you, I will.
Climb the highest mountain there is, until.
Your treasure; my body is breathless.

Trotting up a steep hill is not enough.
A public message of my love takes modest time to do.
It may seem extreme but it is my heart speaking.

I trust you like the supreme above trust his angels.
Placing my left hand in yours to say "I do", I did so.
Feeling the rush of joy down my cheeks, I felt each drop.

You have made life easier to breathe.
Your simplicity and passionate deeds.
I smile gracefully because of you.
You and you only I live for.

Without you close

Numb, lonely.
Tears, raining.
I cannot feel it.
No warmth, believe it.
Us apart is unbearable.
I am lost; weak without you.
You, it is you that I want.
It is you that I need.
I wish for you.
Cry for you.
I yearn for you.
Each day.

Fall Out

My heart is more than willing to converse,
But my mind is baffled as to why we have fallen out.
Over and over again, I feel like I am the one to blame.
I can be too critical at times and I have come to apprehend that fact.
Always over analyzing the words you speak to me.
Negatively thinking when there is no need to.
How do I get myself to pick up the phone and dial your number?
And if I do, how do I start a dialogue with you?
My gut tells me that you are still upset.
Because it is midnight and I haven't receive a call.
"How do I make things feel right?" I asked myself.
I am less angry at you;
I'm here wondering how many more sorry's do I have left.
Why must I be the root of these fights?
Jumping to conclusion, and always aiming to be right.
How stubborn of me! To win what exactly? I do not know.
Do I not know how to compromise?
Or know how to not have my own way?
For just one second, I wish my mind could be free from anger.
Free from blaming myself.
My behaviour was unintentional and I wish that I didn't hurt you.
But I want us to talk; I miss hearing your voice.
I want to know that you still love me.
And if you won't call, I definitely need to be the one to first do so.

Lost in Lust

Like a newborn, I stood there openly,
Nude and cold that is.
Anticipating what is next.
Perhaps, a mischievous smile;
Excitingly showing what I am feeling on the inside.
There he stood, anxiously breathing.
Heart beating rapidly through his chest,
Biting his lips as though they were food,
But it was me who looked greedy once his robe hit the floor.
It was a sight I envisioned but never so sweet.
Never so breath taking; goose bumps appeared each second.
He swept me off my feet, leaving the pink pedals behind.
This was no dream, nor was I fantasizing.
But my mind was empowered by his glory of a new world.
Soothing yet untamed; full of delight.
It is hard to let go of something so alluring.
His spell lures me deeply into his web of lust.
Heat so intense, it was greater than a desert bed.
Abiding by the wants of our bodies.
We allow the covers beneath us to soak.
Our cheeks glow, shining with glee.
Our lips kissed until they are now like cherries,
But the endurance we had was now drained.
We laid there rejuvenating.
Preparing ourselves to be lost in lust once more.

Picture Perfect

A perfect picture I believe we are.
Without a doubt, our tale will travel far.
I always trust that you love me.
You would always say you will never leave me.
What more could I possibly ask for?
But to have you close in my life.
We are picture perfect despite our flaws.
Accepting our inability to be perfect but to be who we are.
Our imperfection is a beauty within the eyes of each other.
We were not loved by another like the way we do.
It will never be the same if I am not adorned by you.
I hope the picture we have created will not be tossed aside,
But to cherish until life is no more.
Why paint an image over one that is so special?
One so distinct to our love and worth holding onto.
Why speak of the word "everlasting" if not intended to do just that?
With you my husband, we have built a perfect picture of true love.
Thus I will never leave you standing, never in this life time.

Song of Love

Thou I sing of love,
Melodies of blues fills my heart completely.
Thou I sing with passion,
Each word echoes alike unwillingly.
Thou I am strong,
I am weak to your absence.
Embracing nothing else but sadness and loneliness.
Mine eyes are heavier than a dark rain cloud.
Raining tears down my cheeks with a warm shower on my back.
Behind these shower curtains, I wish you were present.
To undo the numbness I feel from deep within.
To erase my sorrowful tears and bring tears of joy I missed.
Because I am lost within this song of love, my dear.
Resting my body against this solid tiled wall.
My voice trembles, my lips sealed.
My face buried in the palms of my hands.
I cannot sing no more.
I cannot stand no longer.
My hair getting soaked by the shower is the least to think about.
It is you that I missed; the one that fills my mind.
The more reason to firmly hold onto the true love we share.
Being mindful that the distance will soon be shortened.
For I love thee truly and believe nothing will separate us.
Not even songs of love that bring tears to my eyes.

What is there to consider?

What is there to consider?
But the barriers left unmoved.
Thus the oceans that may never part by my demand,
The mountains that will never stand short to climb,
And the trees that heighten towards the sun.
Nature in its beauty, you could say.
But I wish to gain closeness from my husband day to day.
Once, twice, three times yearly is merely enough.
And so I reminisce of all things that come to mind.
The limited visits that are quick to end soon.
The sudden mood we endure when I leave before noon.
"Safe flight," he would say and "I love you too"
What is there to consider? I think to myself, heartbroken and torn.
The absence of warmth when I lay my head each night,
To reach over beside me and feel nothing but a soft pillow.
No verbal hugs and kisses can cease me
from not wanting you close.
Nor will the goodnight wishes make each night end well.
Yet these signs of reassurance comfort me.
What is there to consider but all.
All that we have been through.
All that we are yet to experience beyond our present life.
Sweetheart I miss you deeply more than you can imagine.
I am cold without you near.
I am not one without you here.
As rested as I am, I see a white cloud appearing above my head.
It is you, eyes closed as you ruminate with me.

One Day

Grateful I am to be the one that you adore,
The love I receive from thee is everlasting and pure.
Assurance is no issue; not by day or by night.
Because being with you grants me no need to distress myself.
Uttering these words, I feel as though we have won.
Compatible indeed; I highly see you as the one.
With years gone by, my commitment gets stronger.
Love feels right because you have loved me unreservedly.
You have made more than a difference in my life.
It is unbearable to patiently wait to have you close.
But sooner or later, either way it will be.

Somehow

In the beginning
I remember seeing myself wanting to be alone.
But every chance I got to take a breath, my phone rang.
I also remember you hanging up in the blink of an eye.
Somehow you could tell by the tone of my voice.
Somehow you could see my body language through the phone.
It was not the same as yours but somehow I did not want to talk.
I missed you yet I felt like being alone.
I argue with you yet I cried after to alleviate the pain.
I meant not to hurt you but somehow my actions
were more vivid than my words. Despite my flaws,
you still managed to love and cope with me.
Somehow this part of our story reversed.
I now want to hear the charming tone of
your voice every second of each day.
I want to share my day with you, my night and even dawn.
I want you to know when I am feeling blue, happy and lonely.
Somehow I found myself wanting to accept this change.
Hence, I would not get to appreciate the relationship that we got.
I maybe would not understand that you are my true better half.
The one I am still with right now.
Somehow we have made it pass the clouds but
I want us to aim further into the sky.

You and I

You and I,
Do you ever wonder why?
Why are we so in love with each other?
Is it that we were just meant to be together?
The times we spare.
The moments we share.
You and I are a matching pair.
With your love and my love, the stronger we get.
With your heart and mines, we share the same love and affection.
You and I,
Do you ever wonder why?
Will we ever part?
Or will we be a perfect heart?

Dear Telesha

Sometimes I wonder if life is really worthy,
Then I look at your smile, I know yes it is.
I love my eyes when you look into them.
I love my name each time you speak it.
And I love my life because you are a part of it.
Maybe you could find someone better than me,
Important than me,
Dearer than me,
But not the one who will love you more than me.

With Love Shawn

Dear Shawn

Sometimes I wonder if the distance between us is really worth it,
Then I look at our journey, I know yes it is.
I love my smile whenever you look at me.
I love my middle name whenever you call me by it.
And I love my life because I get to grow with you.
Maybe someone out there is kinder than me,
Beautiful than me,
Humorous than me,
But not the one who will love, cherish and
appreciate you more than me.

With Love Telesha

Printed in the United States
By Bookmasters